The Day You Were Born
U.K. Yearbook

ISBN: 9798567578995

© Diamond Publishing 2020
All Rights Reserved

	Page
Calendar	5
People in High Office	6
British News & Events	10
Worldwide News & Events	19
Births - U.K. Personalities	26
Notable British Deaths	32
Popular Music	35
Top 5 Films	41
Sporting Winners	52
Cost of Living	60
Cartoons & Comic Strips	69

FIRST EDITION

January	February	March
M T W T F S S	M T W T F S S	M T W T F S S
1 2 3	1 2 3 4 5 6 7	1 2 3 4 5 6 7
4 5 6 7 8 9 10	8 9 10 11 12 13 14	8 9 10 11 12 13 14
11 12 13 14 15 16 17	15 16 17 18 19 20 21	15 16 17 18 19 20 21
18 19 20 21 22 23 24	22 23 24 25 26 27 28	22 23 24 25 26 27 28
25 26 27 28 29 30 31		29 30 31
☽:4 ○:11 ☾:19 ●:26	☽:2 ○:10 ☾:18 ●:25	☽:4 ○:12 ☾:20 ●:26

April	May	June
M T W T F S S	M T W T F S S	M T W T F S S
1 2 3 4	1 2	1 2 3 4 5 6
5 6 7 8 9 10 11	3 4 5 6 7 8 9	7 8 9 10 11 12 13
12 13 14 15 16 17 18	10 11 12 13 14 15 16	14 15 16 17 18 19 20
19 20 21 22 23 24 25	17 18 19 20 21 22 23	21 22 23 24 25 26 27
26 27 28 29 30	24 25 26 27 28 29 30	28 29 30
	31	
☽:2 ○:10 ☾:18 ●:25	☽:2 ○:10 ☾:17 ●:24	☽:1 ○:9 ☾:16 ●:22 ☽:30

July	August	September
M T W T F S S	M T W T F S S	M T W T F S S
1 2 3 4	1	1 2 3 4 5
5 6 7 8 9 10 11	2 3 4 5 6 7 8	6 7 8 9 10 11 12
12 13 14 15 16 17 18	9 10 11 12 13 14 15	13 14 15 16 17 18 19
19 20 21 22 23 24 25	16 17 18 19 20 21 22	20 21 22 23 24 25 26
26 27 28 29 30 31	23 24 25 26 27 28 29	27 28 29 30
	30 31	
○:8 ☾:15 ●:22 ☽:30	○:6 ☾:13 ●:20 ☽:29	○:5 ☾:11 ●:19 ☽:27

October	November	December
M T W T F S S	M T W T F S S	M T W T F S S
1 2 3	1 2 3 4 5 6 7	1 2 3 4 5
4 5 6 7 8 9 10	8 9 10 11 12 13 14	6 7 8 9 10 11 12
11 12 13 14 15 16 17	15 16 17 18 19 20 21	13 14 15 16 17 18 19
18 19 20 21 22 23 24	22 23 24 25 26 27 28	20 21 22 23 24 25 26
25 26 27 28 29 30 31	29 30	27 28 29 30 31
○:4 ☾:11 ●:19 ☽:27	○:2 ☾:9 ●:18 ☽:25	○:2 ☾:9 ●:17 ☽:25 ○:31

People in High Office

Monarch - Queen Elizabeth II
Reign: 6th February 1952 - Present
Predecessor: King George VI
Heir Apparent: Charles, Prince of Wales

United Kingdom

Prime Minister
Edward Heath
Conservative Party
19th June 1970 - 4th March 1974

New Zealand

Ireland

United States

Prime Minister
Keith Holyoake
12th December 1960 -
7th February 1972

Taoiseach
Jack Lynch
10th November 1966 -
14th March 1973

President
Richard Nixon
20th January 1969 -
9th August 1974

Flag	Country	Leader
	Australia	Prime Minister John Gorton (1968-1971) William McMahon (1971-1972)
	Brazil	President Emílio Garrastazú Médici (1969-1974)
	Canada	Prime Minister Pierre Trudeau (1968-1979)
	China	Communist Party Leader Mao Zedong (1935-1976)
	France	President Georges Pompidou (1969-1974)
	India	Prime Minister Indira Gandhi (1966-1977)
	Israel	Prime Minister Golda Meir (1969-1974)
	Italy	Prime Minister Emilio Colombo (1970-1972)

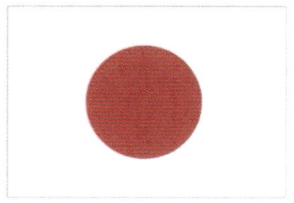	Japan	Prime Minister Eisaku Satō (1964-1972)
	Mexico	President Luis Echeverría Álvarez (1970-1976)
	Pakistan	President Yahya Khan (1969-1971) Zulfikar Ali Bhutto (1971-1973)
	South Africa	Prime Minister B. J. Vorster (1966-1978)
	Soviet Union	Communist Party Leader Leonid Brezhnev (1964-1982)
	Spain	Prime Minister Francisco Franco (1938-1973)
	Turkey	Prime Minister Süleyman Demirel (1965-1971) Nihat Erim (1971-1972)
	West Germany	Chancellor Willy Brandt (1969-1974)

BRITISH NEWS & EVENTS

JAN

1st — The Divorce Reform Act 1969 comes into effect allowing couples to divorce after a separation of two years (five if only one of them agrees). *Notes: A divorce could now also be granted on the grounds that the marriage has irretrievably broken down, and it was no longer essential for either partner to prove "fault". Extra: On the 19th January 1972 it was revealed that the number of divorces in Britain during 1971 had exceeded 100,000 for the first time.*

2nd — Ibrox disaster: A stairway crush at Ibrox Stadium in Glasgow during a Rangers vs. Celtic football match leads to 66 deaths and more than 200 injuries.

3rd — The Open University begins broadcasting on the BBC.

5th — The first ever One Day International cricket match is played between Australia and England at the Melbourne Cricket Ground in Victoria, Australia - Australia wins the game by 5 wickets.

8th — Tupamaros guerrillas kidnap Geoffrey Jackson, the British ambassador to Uruguay, in Montevideo. *Follow up: Jackson was released after 8 months on the 9th September in a deal (costing £42,000) negotiated by Prime Minister Edward Heath.*

12th — The Hertfordshire house of the Secretary of State for Employment Robert Carr is bombed. Nobody is injured.

14th — The extremist group "the Angry Brigade" admit responsibility for the bombing of Robert Carr's house. They also claim to have carried out attacks on the Spanish Embassy in London as well as planting bombs near a BBC van during the Miss World contest and at the Department of Employment offices in Westminster.

14th — The first Commonwealth Heads of Government Meeting is held in Singapore. Hosted by Prime Minister Lee Kuan Yew, the meeting goes on until the 22nd January.

15th — George Harrison releases his first solo single "My Sweet Lord" in the United Kingdom (it would go on to top music charts around the world).

20th — The first ever national postal strike begins after postal workers demand a pay rise of 15-20% and then walk out after Post Office managers make a lower offer. Led by UPW General Secretary Tom Jackson, the 200,000 members remain on strike until the 8th March.

21st — After collapsing in March 1969, the newly reconstructed Emley Moor transmitter in West Yorkshire recommences operation. Now a 1084ft (330.4m) concrete tower, it is Britain's tallest freestanding structure.

23rd — Riots break out in the Shankill Road area of Belfast, North Ireland.

25th — The 170 delegates of the Ulster Unionist Council (UUC) call for the resignation of Northern Ireland Prime Minister James Chichester-Clark.

FEB

— The broadcast receiver licence, first introduced in 1923, is abolished for radios.

3rd — A series of house searches by the British Army in Catholic areas of Belfast result in serious rioting and gun battles.

FEB

4th	Rolls-Royce goes bankrupt and is nationalised.
6th	The Irish Republican Army (IRA) shoots and kills Gunner Robert Curtis, the first British soldier to die during the Troubles.
9th	Five men are killed near a BBC transmitter on Brougher Mountain, County Tyrone, in a landmine attack carried out by the IRA.
11th	A multilateral agreement between the United States, Soviet Union, United Kingdom and 91 other countries is signed banning the emplacement of nuclear weapons or "weapons of mass destruction" on the ocean floor beyond a 12-mile coastal zone.
12th	Leading Australian batsman Ken Eastwood plays in his only Test match in the final match of the Ashes series against England; he scores just 5 runs. *Fun fact: Although Eastwood played only one Test he ended up with two caps. He was given two caps to try for size and no one ever asked him to return the unused one.*
15th	Decimal Day: The United Kingdom and the Republic of Ireland both switch to decimal currency abandoning the £sd (pounds, shillings and pence) system that had been in operation for 1,200 years.
24th	Home Secretary Reginald Maudling announces the Immigration Bill that is set to strip Commonwealth immigrants of their right to remain in the United Kingdom.

MAR

1st	Hundreds of thousands of workers across Britain take part in an unofficial day of protest against the government's new Industrial Relations Act.
5th	Led Zeppelin play their iconic rock anthem "Stairway to Heaven" live for the first time at Ulster Hall in Belfast. *Fun fact: Bassist John Paul Jones later recalled that the crowd was unimpressed: "They were all bored to tears waiting to hear something they knew".*
8th	The postal workers' strike ends after 47 days.
12th	In response to the killing by the IRA of three off-duty Scottish soldiers, Dougald McCaughey (23), Joseph McCaig (18) and John McCaig (17), thousands of Belfast shipyard workers march demanding the introduction of Internment for members of the Irish Republican Army.
16th	Northern Ireland Prime Minister James Chichester-Clark meets with Prime Minister Edward Heath to discuss the security situation in Northern Ireland. An additional 1,300 troops are sent to the region.
20th	James Chichester-Clark resigns as Northern Ireland Prime Minister in protest of what he views as the limited security response by the British government.
20th	Tom Jones' single "She's a Lady" reaches No.2 on the Billboard Hot 100 Chart. *Fun fact: It is Jones' highest-charting single to date in the United States.*
23rd	Brian Faulkner succeeds as Northern Ireland Prime Minister after defeating William Craig in a Unionist Party leadership election.

APR

1st	The United Kingdom lifts all restrictions on gold ownership. *NB: Since 1966 Britons had been banned from holding more than four gold coins unless they held a licence.*

APR

1st	The first two members of the Rolling Stones, Bill Wyman and Mick Taylor, leave England for France to escape the 90% higher rate of income tax. Keith Richards, Charlie Watts and Mick Jagger follow two days later.
18th	A serious fire closes Kentish Town West railway station. *NB: It does not re-open until the 5th October 1981.*
27th	Eight members of the Welsh Language Society go on trial for destroying English language road signs in Wales.

27th April: British Leyland launch the Morris Marina to serve as a replacement for the Morris Minor which had been in production since 1948. Intended to compete with the Ford Cortina, Vauxhall Victor and Hillman Hunter, it has 1.3 and 1.8 litre petrol engines and a choice of four-door family saloon, and two-door coupé body styles (a five-door estate is set to follow within two years). *Notes: Frequently described by journalists, authors and motoring critics as one of the worst cars of all time, it was nevertheless a popular car in Britain throughout its production life and was exported around world. NB: Of the 807,000 Marinas sold in Britain it was reported in February 2016 that the number still on Britain's roads was 295, making it the most-scrapped car sold in Britain over the previous 30 years.* Photo: Prospective buyers looking at a new Morris Marina.

MAY

1st	A bomb planted by the Angry Brigade explodes in the Biba boutique in Kensington High Street, West London. Around 500 people are evacuated from the store but no-one is seriously hurt.
3rd	The Daily Mail is relaunched as a tabloid newspaper after 75 years as a broadsheet.

MAY

3rd	Arsenal F.C. wins the English Division 1 football league championship at the home of their bitter rivals, Tottenham Hotspur; Tottenham 0-1 Arsenal.
8th	Arsenal win the FA Cup final with a 2-1 win over Liverpool at Wembley Stadium to complete the Football League First Division and the FA Cup double.
11th	The Daily Sketch, Britain's oldest tabloid newspaper, is withdrawn from circulation after 62 years and is absorbed by the new look Daily Mail.
15th	William 'Billy' Reid, an IRA member, is shot dead by British soldiers in Belfast. *Notes: According to 'Lost Lives' Reid was the person who fired the shot which killed Robert Curtis, the first British soldier to be killed in the Troubles on the 6th February 1971.*
21st	Chelsea F.C., the previous year's FA Cup winners, win the European Cup Winners' Cup with a 2-1 victory over Real Madrid in Athens.
23rd	Aviogenex Flight 130, carrying mainly British tourists from Gatwick Airport to Rijeka Airport, Yugoslavia, suffers a structural failure during landing and crashes killing 78 of the 83 people onboard.
25th	British Army Sergeant Michael Willetts is killed and seven officers wounded in an IRA bomb attack on the joint Royal Ulster Constabulary / British Army base on the Springfield Road in Belfast.

JUN

7th	The BBC's children's show Blue Peter buries a time capsule in the grounds of Television Centre (it is due to be opened on the first show of the year 2000).
13th	In defiance of a government ban, 2,000 members of the Orange Order march through the mainly Catholic town of Dungiven, County Londonderry.

14th June: Americans Isaac Tigrett and Peter Morton open the first Hard Rock Cafe near Hyde Park Corner in London. *Fun facts: As of July 2018, Hard Rock International has venues in 74 countries, including 185 cafes, 25 hotels and 12 casinos.*

14th	Education Secretary Margaret Thatcher's proposals to end free school milk for children aged over seven years old are backed by a majority of 33 MPs. *Notes: Edward Short, the Labour Secretary of State for Education and Science, had withdrawn free milk from secondary schools in 1968. Shirley Williams eventually abolished free milk completely (for the remaining under sevens) in 1977.*
15th	In reaction to Thatcher's plans several Labour run councils threaten to increase rates in order to continue the free supply of milk to school children aged over seven years. Thatcher defends her plans saying that the change will free up more money to be spent on the construction of new school buildings.
15th	The Scottish shipbuilding consortium Upper Clyde Shipbuilders enters liquidation.
19th	The television chat show "Parkinson" debuts on BBC1. *Fun facts: Presented by Michael Parkinson the show ran for 31 series and 540 episodes (until the 22nd December 2007).*
20th	Government officials announce that Soviet space scientist Anatoly Fedoseyev (who had defected the previous month during a visit to the Paris Air Show) is in Britain and has been granted asylum.
21st	The Heath Government begins new negotiations in Luxembourg in an attempt to gain membership of the European Economic Community.

25th June: The first Reading Festival takes place over a period of three days as part of the town's 1971 Festival of Arts. With a weekend ticket costing £2, and starring the likes of Arthur Brown, East of Eden, Coliseum, Lindisfarne and Genesis, the event proved very popular. *Fun facts: The Reading Festival was originally known as the National Jazz Festival and was conceived by Harold Pendleton (founder of the Marquee Club in London in 1958) and first held at Richmond Athletic Ground in 1961. Today it is the world's oldest popular music festival still in existence and has hosted some of the world's biggest bands over the past five decades.*

1st	John Schlesinger's film Sunday Bloody Sunday is released; it is one of the first mainstream British films with a bisexual theme.
6th	Police launch a murder investigation after three French tourists are found shot dead in Cheshire.
8th	During street disturbances in Derry, Northern Ireland, rioters Seamus Cusack and Desmond Beattie are shot dead by British troops.
14th	Michael Bassett, aged 24, is found dead in his fume-filled car in Staffordshire. Police have identified him as their prime suspect in the recent triple French tourist murder in Cheshire.
16th	The Social Democratic and Labour Party (SDLP) withdraw from Stormont because no official inquiry has been announced into the killings of Seamus Cusack and Desmond Beattie (8th July).

23rd July: Princess Alexandra opens the second phase of the Victoria London Underground line before boarding a train from Brixton to Vauxhall. *Notes: It is the first new section of Underground to open south of the Thames since the extension of the City and South London Railway from Clapham Common to Morden in 1926.*

29th	The Minister of State for Trade and Industry, Frederick Corfield, announces the cancellation of the Black Arrow satellite carrier rocket project in the House of Commons. *Follow up: As the (R3) Black Arrow rocket had already been shipped to the launch site, permission was given for that flight to go ahead (28th October).*
30th	Upper Clyde Shipbuilders workers begin to take control of the shipyards in a work-in under the leadership of Jimmy Reid. Reid, along with his colleagues Jimmy Airlie, Sammy Gilmore and Sammy Barr, had decided that the best way to show the viability of keeping the yards open was by staging a 'work-in' rather than by going on strike.

AUG

3rd	Paul McCartney announces formation of his new band; the group are named "Wings" on the 9th October.

6th August: Former paratrooper Chay Blyth, aboard the 59-foot yacht British Steel, becomes the first person to sail non-stop westwards around the world (against the prevailing winds and currents). *Notes: The achievement took 292 days and resulted in him being made a Commander of the Order of the British Empire (CBE). Photos: Chay Blyth aboard British Steel / Meeting Prince Philip, Prince Charles, Princess Anne, wife Maureen and daughter Samantha after his historic voyage.*

9th	Operation Demetrius (or Internment) is introduced in Northern Ireland allowing suspected terrorists to be indefinitely detained without trial; the security forces arrest 342 people suspected of supporting paramilitaries. There is an immediate upsurge of violence and 17 people are killed during the next 48 hours.
10th	Mr. Tickle, the first book in the Mr. Men series (written and illustrated by Roger Hargreaves) is first published. *Fun facts: As of 2015 a total of 85 Mr. Men and Little Miss characters have been featured in the series, which has included sales of over 100 million books worldwide, across 28 countries.*
11th	Prime Minister Edward Heath steers the British Admiral's Cup team to victory at the helm of his 42-foot yacht Morning Cloud.
14th	The Who release their critically acclaimed album Who's Next. *Notes: The recording is viewed by many critics as the Who's best record and one of the greatest albums of all time.*
15th	Bahrain proclaims independence after 110 years of British rule (it formally gains its independence as the State of Bahrain on the 16th December 1971).
15th	Harvey Smith is stripped of his victory and £2,000 winnings for making a V sign at the British Show Jumping Derby. *Follow up: Amid huge publicity and public backing his disqualification is reversed two days later.*
15th	Despite crashing out on lap 36, Scotsman Jackie Stewart clinches his second Formula 1 World Drivers Championship at the Austrian Grand Prix at the Österreichring.
16th	Over 8,000 workers go on strike in Derry, Northern Ireland, in protest at the introduction of Internment.
31st	John Lennon leaves England for New York, never to return.

SEP

1st	The pre-decimal penny and threepence coins cease to be legal tender.
1st	Qatar declares independence from the United Kingdom (it formally becomes an independent state two days later).
6th	Prime Minister Edward Heath meets with the Irish Taoiseach Jack Lynch at Chequers to discuss the situation in Northern Ireland.
6th	William Craig and Ian Paisley speak at a rally in Belfast, before a crowd of 20,000 people, and call for the establishment of a third force to defend 'Ulster'.
6th	After three years of conflict in Northern Ireland 14-year-old Annette McGavigan becomes the 100th civilian to be killed in the Troubles. She is fatally wounded by a gunshot in crossfire between British soldiers and the IRA.
21st	The television music show The Old Grey Whistle Test is aired for the first time on BBC 2.
24th	Following revelations made after the defection of top KGB officer Oleg Lyalin from the Soviet Embassy, Britain expels 105 Russian diplomats for spying.
27th	Tripartite talks involving the prime ministers of Northern Ireland, Britain and the Taoiseach of the Republic of Ireland take place at Chequers.
30th	The Democratic Unionist Party (DUP) is founded by the Reverend Ian Paisley in Northern Ireland. Paisley would go on to lead the party for the next 37 years.

OCT

1st	Godfrey Hounsfield's invention, the CAT scan, was used for the first time on a patient with a cerebral cyst at Atkinson Morley Hospital in Wimbledon.
7th	Northern Ireland Prime Minister Brian Faulkner meets with British Prime Minister Edward Heath and his Cabinet. The meeting sees an additional 1,500 troops being sent to Northern Ireland.
21st	A gas explosion in the town centre of Clarkston, East Renfrewshire, kills 22 people and injures around 100.
21st	The television drama Edna, the Inebriate Woman is first shown on BBC One. The play gains an audience of some 29.25 million and sees Patricia Hayes receive the award for Best Actress at the 1972 British Academy Television Awards.
23rd	Two female members of the IRA are shot dead by soldiers in the Lower Falls area of Belfast after their car fails to stop at a checkpoint.
28th	The House of Commons votes 356-244 in favour of joining the European Economic Community.
28th	The Immigration Act 1971, restricting immigration, particularly primary immigration into the United Kingdom, and introducing the concept of right of abode, receives royal assent.
28th	The United Kingdom becomes the sixth nation successfully to launch a satellite (the Prospero X-3 experimental communications satellite) into orbit. Using a Black Arrow carrier rocket from Woomera Launch Area 5 in South Australia, it is the first and only successful orbital launch to be conducted by the United Kingdom.
31st	The IRA explode a bomb at the Post Office Tower in London. *Notes: At the time part of the tower was open to members of the public and was a London tourist attraction. The public area was closed following the attack and did not reopen.*

NOV

	Erin Pizzey establishes Chiswick Women's Aid (now known as Refuge), the world's first domestic violence shelter.
9th	A Royal Air Force C-130 Hercules crashes into the Ligurian Sea near Livorno, Italy, killing all 46 passengers and 6 crew.
10th	The 10-route Gravelly Hill Interchange (otherwise known as Spaghetti Junction) opens north of Birmingham city centre. *Notes: The interchange had a total of 12 routes when it was officially opened by Peter Walker, the Secretary of State for the Environment, on the 24th May 1972.*
22nd	In Britain's worst mountaineering tragedy (the Cairngorm Plateau Disaster) five children and one of their leaders are found dead from exposure after becoming stranded for two nights in a blizzard in the Scottish mountains.

DEC

2nd	The United Arab Emirates declares its independence from United Kingdom.
4th	Fifteen Catholic civilians are killed when Loyalist paramilitaries explode a bomb at The Tramore Bar, better known as McGurk's bar, in North Queen Street, north Belfast. *NB: This is the highest death toll from a single incident in Belfast during the Troubles.*
10th	Hungarian-British electrical engineer and physicist Dennis Gabor wins the Nobel Prize in Physics "for his invention and development of the holographic method".
16th	The Banking and Financial Dealings Act is passed amending and updating the definition of bank holidays within the United Kingdom.
23rd	Prime Minister Edward Heath visits Northern Ireland and expresses his determination to end the violence
30th	The seventh James Bond film, Diamonds Are Forever, is released. Sean Connery, who appeared in the first five films before being succeeded by George Lazenby for On Her Majesty's Secret Service in 1969, returns to the role for one final appearance in the official series of films.
31st	The inflation rate in the United Kingdom for 1971 is 9.44%, up from 6.4% in 1970.

1971 BRITISH PUBLICATIONS

The Destiny Waltz - Gerda Charles (winner of the first Whitbread Award for fiction)
Nemesis (Miss Marple) - Agatha Christie
Maurice - E. M. Forster (posthumous)
The Day of the Jackal - Frederick Forsyth
Mr. Tickle - Roger Hargreaves (first of the Mr. Men series)
Adolf Hitler: My Part in His Downfall - Spike Milligan
In a Free State - V. S. Naipaul
The Carpet People - Terry Pratchett
The Towers of Silence - Paul Scott (third of the Raj Quartet)
Religion and the Decline of Magic - Keith Thomas

60 WORLDWIDE NEWS & EVENTS

1. 2nd January: The Public Health Cigarette Smoking Act (signed by President Nixon on the 1st April 1970) comes into effect banning cigarette advertisements on radio and television in the United States.
2. 15th January: Egyptian President Anwar el-Sadat and Nikolai Podgorny, the Soviet chief of state, officially open the billion-dollar Aswan High Dam in Egypt.
3. 16th January: Dutch skater Ard Schenk skates a world record 1500m in a time of 1m 58.7s; Schenk is the first to skate the distance in under 2 minutes.
4. 18th January: Ivan Koloff defeats Bruno Sammartino for the WWWF World Heavyweight Wrestling Championship. *Notes: Italian Superman Sammartino had held the title since the 17th May 1963, the longest in the Championships history.*
5. 25th January: In Uganda, Idi Amin deposes Milton Obote in a military coup and declares himself president.
6. 31st January: Apollo 14, carrying astronauts Alan Shepard, Stuart Roosa and Edgar Mitchell, lifts off from Launch Complex 39-A at Cape Canaveral, Florida. Their ten-day mission will be the third successful lunar landing mission, the eighth crewed mission in the United States Apollo program, and the first to land in the lunar highlands. *Fun facts: Commander Alan Shepard was one of the original NASA Mercury Seven astronauts selected in 1959. He was the first American to travel into space and is so far the only person to hit a golf ball on the Moon.*
7. 4th February: The NASDAQ stock exchange, now the second-largest in the world behind the New York Stock Exchange, is founded in New York City.
8. 7th February: Switzerland votes for national women's suffrage in a referendum.
9. 16th February: At President Richard Nixon's request a secret taping system is installed in the Oval Office and Cabinet Room in the White House.

10. 28th February: Stunt performer and entertainer Evel Knievel sets a new world record by jumping 19 cars (18 Dodge Colts and a van) with his Harley-Davidson XR-750 at the Ontario Motor Speedway in California.

11.	3rd March: After 5 years of censorship the South African Broadcasting Corporation lifts its ban on the Beatles.
12.	7th March: Sheikh Mujibur Rahman, the founding father of Bangladesh and the then political leader of East Pakistan, delivers a speech at the Ramna Race Course in Dhaka to a gathering of over two million people. In it he calls on the masses to be prepared to fight for national independence.
13.	8th March: In the "Fight of the Century" Joe Frazier ends Muhammad Ali's 31-fight winning streak at Madison Square Garden, New York, to retain his heavyweight boxing title by a unanimous points decision.
14.	12th March: Hafez al-Assad consolidates power in Syria by installing himself as President. *NB: Assad would remain in power until his death 3 decades later on the 10th June 2000.*
15.	16th March: The 13th Grammy Awards, recognising the accomplishments of musicians during 1970, are held at the Hollywood Palladium in Los Angeles. The winners include Simon and Garfunkel for "Bridge over Troubled Water", and Best New Artist, The Carpenters.
16.	18th March: A landslide into Lake Yanahuani in Peru creates a wave 30 metres high which destroys the Chungar Mine camp and kills over 200 miners.
17.	26th March: Bangladesh declares its independence from Pakistan; a nine-month guerrilla war ensues which results in the deaths of over 300,000 people.
18.	3rd April: At the 16th Eurovision Song Contest in Dublin, Severine wins for Monaco singing "Un banc, un arbre, une rue".
19.	5th April: Canadian Frances Phipps becomes the first woman to reach North Pole.

20. 15th April: The 43rd Academy Awards, to honour the best films of 1970, takes place at the Dorothy Chandler Pavilion in Los Angeles, California. The winners include the epic biographical war film Patton, and actors George C Scott and Glenda Jackson. *Pictured: Best Actress Glenda Jackson / Producer Frank McCarthy appearing on behalf of Best Actor George C. Scott. Note: The next day Scott refused his Oscar (the first actor to do so) and McCarthy returned it to the Academy.*

21.	19th April: The USSR launch Salyut 1, the first space station launched into low Earth orbit.

22.	19th April: At the Tate-LaBianca murder trial in Los Angeles, California, Judge Charles H. Older sentences cult leader Charles Manson to death and he is ordered sent to San Quentin's death row. *Follow up: The sentence for all California death row inmates was commuted to life imprisonment in 1972 - Manson remained incarcerated until his death, aged 83, on November 19, 2017.*
23.	22nd April: Soyuz 10 launches as the world's first mission to the first-ever space station (Salyut 1). The docking procedure however is unsuccessful and the cosmonauts return to Earth.

24. 24th April: An estimated 500,000 people in Washington, D.C. march to demand an end to the war in Vietnam. The crowd includes several members of the United States Congress, but none of the prospective presidential candidates for 1972. Additionally, in San Francisco, 150,000 march for the same cause. The rallies are sponsored by the National Peace Action Coalition.

25.	5th May: The U.S. dollar floods the European currency markets threatening the Deutsche Mark; the central banks of Austria, Belgium, Netherlands and Switzerland stop all dollar trades.
26.	19th May: The USSR launches the space probe Mars 2. *Notes: The Mars 2 lander became the first human-made object to reach the surface of Mars after crash landing on the planet on the 27th November 1971. The Mars 2 orbiter continued to circle Mars and transmit images back to Earth for another nine months.*
27.	27th May: At the 24th Cannes Film Festival "The Go-Between", directed by Joseph Losey, wins the Grand Prix du Festival International du Film (now called the Palme d'Or).
28.	28th May: The USSR launches the space probe Mars 3. *Notes: The Mars 3 lander became the first spacecraft to soft land on Mars on the 2nd December 1971 (although it failed 110 seconds after landing). Like the Mars 2 orbiter, the Mars 3 orbiter successfully transmitted images back to Earth until August 1972.*
29.	2nd June: Ajax beats Panathinaikos 2-0 at Wembley Stadium to win the European Cup; the Dutch champions would go on win it again in both 1972 and 1973.

30. 3rd June: The Eighteen-year-old future Prime Minister of Pakistan, Imran Khan, makes his Test cricket debut against England at Edgbaston. *Fun facts: Khan took over the captaincy of the Pakistan cricket team from Javed Miandad in 1982 and was the captain of the national team that won the 1992 Cricket World Cup.*
31. 6th June: Soyuz 11, carrying cosmonauts Georgy Dobrovolsky, Vladislav Volkov, and Viktor Patsayevto, takes off toward the Salyut 1 space station. It docks successfully the following day but the mission ends in disaster on the 29th June during their return to Earth. The crew capsule depressurises during preparations for re-entry killing the three-man crew (they are the only humans known to have died in space).
32. 10th June: The United States ends a 21-year embargo on trade with Communist China.
33. 3rd July: Twenty-seven-year old Jim Morrison, the lead singer and lyricist of The Doors, is found dead in his bathtub in Paris, France.
34. 18th July: Eddy Merckx of Belgium wins the 58th Tour de France, his third straight victory (he would go on to win it again on two further occasions in 1972 and 1974).
35. 19th July: The South Tower of the World Trade Center in New York is topped out at 1,362 feet, making it the second tallest building in the world; the North Tower, standing 1,368 feet (topped out on the 23rd December 1970), is the tallest.

36. 26th July: Apollo 15, carrying astronauts David Scott, Alfred Worden and James Irwin, is launched from the Kennedy Space Center at Merritt Island, Florida. Their twelve-day mission will be the fourth successful lunar landing mission and the first to use the Lunar Roving Vehicle. *Fun facts: The Apollo 15 mission is notable for the discovery of the Genesis Rock, for Scott's use of a hammer and a feather to validate Galileo's theory that objects fall at the same rate in the absence of air resistance, and for Command Module Pilot Alfred Worden performing the first spacewalk in deep space. Pictured: James Irwin salutes the United States flag on the Moon (2nd August).*

37.	30th July: A Japan Air Self-Defense Force F-86F Sabre jet fighter collides with a Boeing 727 airliner en route from Sapporo to Tokyo. The Sabre pilot, a trainee, is the only survivor, all 162 occupants on the 727 are killed.
38.	1st August: At Madison Square Garden in New York City, 40,000 attend the Concert for Bangladesh, a pair of benefit concerts organised by former Beatles guitarist George Harrison and Indian sitar player Ravi Shankar.
39.	18th August: Australia and New Zealand announce that they are to withdraw their troops from Vietnam before the end of the year.
40.	2nd September: Teenage debutants Chris Evert (16) and Jimmy Connors (19th birthday) win their first matches at the U.S. Open Tennis Championships at the West Side Tennis Club in Forest Hills, New York. *Fun facts: Evert would go on to win 18 Grand Slam singles championships, and Connors would win 8.*
41.	18th September: Taiwanese-Japanese inventor and businessman Momofuku Ando markets the first Cup Noodle. The product inspires numerous competing products such as the Pot Noodle brand in the United Kingdom (launched by Golden Wonder in 1977).
42.	29th September: A cyclone and tidal wave off the Bay of Bengal kills as many as 10,000 people.

43. 1st October: Magic Kingdom opens at the Walt Disney World Resort near the cities of Orlando and Kissimmee in Florida. Admission prices are $3.50 for adults, $2.50 for juniors under the age of 18, and $1 for children under twelve. *Fun facts: Today Walt Disney World has over 77,000 employees and is the most visited holiday resort in the world (with an average annual attendance of more than 58 million). Pictured: Walt Disney World group photo just prior to the grand opening of the amusement park.*

44.	1st October: The Dutch politician and diplomat Joseph Luns is appointed as the secretary-general of NATO; he serves in the post until the 25th June 1984.
45.	5th October: Emperor Hirohito and Empress Masako of Japan are welcomed by the Queen and members of the Royal Family at the start of their State Visit to Britain.
46.	7th October: The action-thriller film The French Connection, directed by William Friedkin and starring Gene Hackman, Roy Scheider and Fernando Rey, premieres in the United States. *NB: It would go on to win the Oscar for Best Picture at the 44th Academy Awards in Los Angeles on the 10th April 1972.*
47.	12th - 16th October: An elaborate set of festivities take place in Iran to celebrate the 2,500-year anniversary of the birth of Persia.
48.	20th October: U.S. Senator Edward Kennedy calls for a withdrawal of troops from Northern Ireland and all-party negotiations to establish a United Ireland.
49.	24th October: American archer and bowyer Harry Drake sets the world record for the longest shot with a footbow (1 mile 268 yards).

50. 14th November: The robotic space probe Mariner 9 (launched toward Mars from LC-36B at Cape Canaveral Air Force Station, Florida, on the 30th May 1971) becomes the first spacecraft to orbit another planet, narrowly beating the Soviet probes Mars 2 and Mars 3 which both arrive just a few weeks later. *Fun facts: Mariner 9 successfully returned 7329 images over the course of its mission, which concluded on the 27th October 1972. Pictured: The Mariner 9 spacecraft.*

51.	15th November: Intel releases the world's first commercially available microprocessor, the Intel 4004.
52.	3rd December: The Indo-Pakistani War of 1971 begins with Operation Chengiz Khan as the Pakistan Air Force launches surprise pre-emptive strikes on eleven airfields in north-western India. Indian Prime Minister Indira Gandhi orders the immediate mobilisation of troops and launches a full-scale invasion of Pakistan.
53.	4th December: The Montreux Casino in Switzerland burns down during a Frank Zappa, Mothers of Invention, concert when a flare, set off by an audience member, starts a fire (the event is immortalised in the Deep Purple song "Smoke on the Water"). The casino is rebuilt in 1975.

54.	10th December: West German Chancellor Willy Brandt is awarded the Nobel Peace Prize in Oslo, Norway.
55.	16th December: The Bangladesh Liberation War ends after the Pakistan Army in East Pakistan surrenders to the joint forces of India and the Bengali nationalist separatists.
56.	20th December: Two groups of French doctors involved in humanitarian aid merge to form Médecins Sans Frontières. *Notes: In 2019, the group was active in 70 countries (with over 35,000 personnel) and had an annual budget of approximately US$1.63 billion.*
57.	24th December: Peruvian LANSA Flight 508 crashes in a thunderstorm en route from Lima to Pucallpa in Peru. Of the 92 crew and passengers on board the only survivor is 17-year-old Juliane Koepcke who, while strapped to her seat, falls 2,800m (9,200ft) into the Amazon rainforest. After surviving the fall, she then walks through the jungle for 11 days before being rescued by local lumbermen.
58.	25th December: A fire at the 22-story Daeyeonggak Hotel in Seoul, South Korea, kills 164 people and injures 63. It remains the deadliest hotel fire in world history.
59.	28th December: Ajax forward Johan Cruyff wins the Ballon d'Or award, for best European football player, ahead of Inter Milan forward Sandro Mazzola, and Manchester United winger George Best; Cruyff is first Dutch national to win award.
60.	30th December: McDonald's Australia opens its first restaurant in the Sydney suburb of Yagoona. *Fun facts: The restaurant becomes known locally as "Maccas" and is the first McDonald's in the Southern Hemisphere. Today there are over 970 McDonald's restaurants across Australia employing more than 100,000 people.*

BIRTHS

British Personalities

BORN IN 1971

Sarah Alexander
b. 3rd January 1971

Actress.

Gary Barlow, OBE
b. 20th January 1971

Singer, songwriter, record producer, actor and television personality (Take That).

Clare Balding, OBE
b. 29th January 1971

Broadcaster, journalist and author.

Patrick Kielty
b. 31st January 1971

Comedian and television personality.

Michelle Gayle

b. 2nd February 1971

Singer, songwriter, actress and author.

Damian Lewis, OBE

b. 11th February 1971

Actor and producer.

Sonia Evans

b. 13th February 1971

Pop singer and actress known mononymously as Sonia.

Amanda Holden

b. 16th February 1971

Media personality, actress, television presenter, singer and author.

Melinda Messenger

b. 23rd February 1971

Television presenter, former glamour model and Page Three girl.

Penny Lancaster

b. 15th March 1971

Model, photographer and TV personality married to rock singer Rod Stewart.

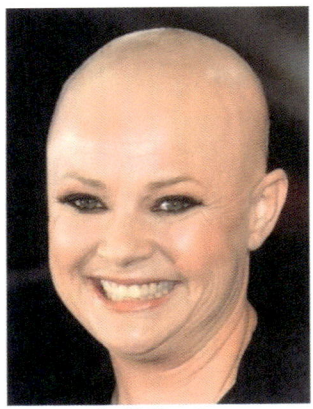

Gail Porter
b. 23rd March 1971

Television presenter and personality, former model and actress.

David Coulthard, MBE
b. 27th March 1971

Former racing driver turned presenter, commentator and journalist.

Ewan McGregor, OBE
b. 31st March 1971

Actor and ambassador for UNICEF UK.

David Tennant
b. 18th April 1971

Actor.

Edd China
b. 9th May 1971

Presenter, mechanic, motor specialist and inventor.

George Osborne, CH
b. 23rd May 1971

Politician and newspaper editor who served as Chancellor of the Exchequer.

Paul Bettany
b. 27th May 1971

British-American actor.

Lee Sharpe
b. 27th May 1971

Former footballer, sports television pundit and reality television personality.

Scott Maslen
b. 25th June 1971

Actor and model.

David Walliams, OBE
b. 20th August 1971

Comedian, actor, writer and television personality.

Gaynor Faye
b. 26th August 1971

Actress and writer.

Kirstie Allsopp
b. 31st August 1971

Television presenter.

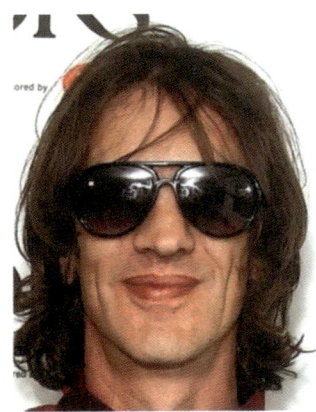

Richard Ashcroft
b. 11th September 1971

Singer and songwriter (The Verve).

Stella McCartney, OBE
b. 13th September 1971

Fashion designer.

Chesney Hawkes
b. 22nd September 1971

Pop singer, songwriter and occasional actor.

Jessie Wallace
b. 25th September 1971

Actress best known for playing Kat Slater in EastEnders.

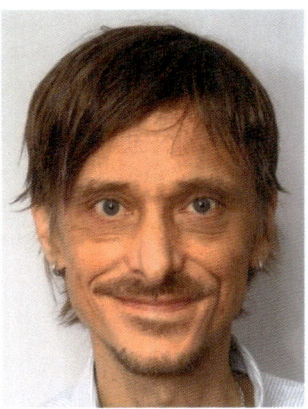

Mackenzie Crook
b. 29th September 1971

Actor, director, comedian and writer.

Sacha Baron Cohen
b. 13th October 1971

Comedian, actor, writer and producer.

Andy Cole
b. 15th October 1971

Former footballer notably remembered for his time with Manchester United.

Craig Phillips
b. 16th October 1971

Television personality and builder (winner of the first series of Big Brother in 2000).

Emily Mortimer
b. 1st December 1971

Actress and screenwriter.

Tara Palmer-Tomkinson
b. 23rd December 1971
d. 8th February 2017

Socialite and television personality.

Dido
b. 25th December 1971

Singer and songwriter born Florian Cloud de Bounevialle Armstrong.

Duncan Ferguson
b. 27th December 1971

Former footballer.

Notable British Deaths

12th Jan	Admiral of the Fleet John Cronyn Tovey, 1st Baron Tovey, GCB, KBE, DSO (b. 7th March 1885) - Royal Navy officer who served as Commander-in-Chief of the Home Fleet and was responsible for orchestrating the pursuit and destruction of the Bismarck.
24th Jan	St. John Greer Ervine (b. 28th December 1883) - Northern Irish biographer, novelist, critic, dramatist and theatre manager.
25th Jan	Donald Woods Winnicott, FRCP (b. 7th April 1896) - Paediatrician and psychoanalyst who was especially influential in the field of object relations theory and developmental psychology.
7th Mar	Florence Margaret Smith (b. 20th September 1902) - Poet and novelist otherwise known as Stevie Smith.
9th Mar	Anthony Berkeley Cox (b. 5th July 1893) - Crime writer who wrote under several pen-names including Francis Iles, Anthony Berkeley and A. Monmouth Platts.
11th Mar	Charlie Dunbar Broad (b. 30th December 1887) - Epistemologist, historian of philosophy, philosopher of science, moral philosopher, and writer on the philosophical aspects of psychical research.
20th Apr	Cecil Parker (b. Cecil Schwabe; 3rd September 1897) - Character and comedy actor who appeared in 91 films between 1928 and 1969.
22nd Apr	Marshal of the Royal Air Force Charles Frederick Algernon Portal, 1st Viscount Portal of Hungerford, KG, GCB, OM, DSO & Bar, MC, DL (b. 21st May 1893) - Senior Royal Air Force officer.

11th May: Lilian Bland (b. 28th September 1878) - Anglo-Irish journalist and pioneer aviator who in 1910 became one of the first women in the world to design, build and fly an aircraft, the Bland Mayfly. *Pictured: Lilian Bland aboard the Bland Mayfly (1910).*

20th May	Waldo Goronwy Williams (b. 30th September 1904) - One of the leading Welsh-language poets of the 20th century. He was also a notable Christian pacifist, anti-war campaigner and Welsh nationalist.
6th Jun	Edward Neville da Costa Andrade, FRS (b. 27th December 1887) - Physicist, writer and poet.
10th Jun	Michael Rennie (b. Eric Alexander Rennie; 25th August 1909) - Film, television and stage actor whose career spanned more than 30 years.

11th June: Benjamin Baruch Ambrose (b. 11th September 1896) - Bandleader and violinist who, in the 1930s, was the leader of the highly acclaimed dance band, Bert Ambrose and his Orchestra. *Pictured: Bert Ambrose and his Orchestra (with the Rhythm Sisters) circa 1935.*

16th Jun	John Charles Walsham Reith, 1st Baron Reith, KT, GCVO, GBE, CB, TD, PC (b. 20th July 1889) - Scottish broadcasting executive who established the tradition of independent public service broadcasting in the United Kingdom.
25th Jun	John Boyd Orr, 1st Baron Boyd-Orr, CH, DSO, MC, FRS, FRSE (b. 23rd September 1880) - Scottish teacher, medical doctor, biologist, nutritional physiologist, politician, businessman and farmer who was awarded the Nobel Peace Prize for his scientific research into nutrition, and his work as the first Director-General of the United Nations Food and Agriculture Organisation (FAO).
1st Jul	Sir William Lawrence Bragg, CH, OBE, MC, FRS (b. 31st March 1890) - Australian-born British physicist and X-ray crystallographer who was the joint recipient (with his father, William Henry Bragg) of the Nobel Prize in Physics in 1915.
4th Jul	Sir Cecil Maurice Bowra, CH, FBA (b. 8th April 1898) - Classical scholar, literary critic and academic.
19th Jul	Lieutenant-Colonel John Jacob Astor V, 1st Baron Astor of Hever, DL (b. 20th May 1886) - American-born English newspaper proprietor, politician, sportsman and military officer.
27th Jul	Charles Patrick Tully (b. 11th July 1924) - Football player and manager who played for Celtic and Northern Ireland.

18th Aug	Lieutenant Colonel Robert Peter Fleming, OBE, DL (b. 31st May 1907) - Adventurer, journalist, soldier and travel writer; he was the elder brother of Ian Fleming, creator of James Bond.
28th Aug	Geoffrey Lawrence, 3rd Baron Trevethin, 1st Baron Oaksey, DSO, PC, DL, TD (b. 2nd December 1880) - The main British judge during the Nuremberg trials after World War II, and President of the Judicial group.
3rd Sep	Percy Holmes (b. 25th November 1886) - First-class cricketer who played for Yorkshire and England.
14th Sep	William Henry Copson (b. 27th April 1908) - First-class cricketer who played for Derbyshire and England.
26th Sep	Air Marshal Sir Robert Henry Magnus Spencer Saundby, KCB, KBE, MC, DFC, AFC, FRAeS, DL (b. 26th April 1896) - Senior Royal Air Force officer whose career spanned both the First and Second World Wars.
3rd Oct	Charles Walter Simpson, RI (b. 8th May 1885) - Painter whose work was exhibited at the Royal Academy of Arts in 1948, and was part of the art competitions at four Olympic Games.
11th Nov	Sir Alan Patrick Herbert, CH (b. 24th September 1890) - Humourist, novelist, playwright and law reform activist who was an Independent Member of Parliament for Oxford University from 1935 until 1950 (when university constituencies were abolished).
17th Nov	Dame Gladys Constance Cooper, DBE (b. 18th December 1888) - Actress whose career spanned seven decades on stage, in films and on television.
7th Dec	Milton Rosmer (b. 4th November 1881) - Actor, film director and screenwriter.
9th Dec	Reverend Aeneas Francon Williams, FRSGS (b. 17th February 1886) - Minister of the Church of Scotland, missionary, Chaplain, writer and poet.
12th Dec	John Eccles Nixon Barnhill (b. 11th April 1905) - Ulster Unionist Party member of the Senate in the Parliament of Northern Ireland.
12th Dec	Alan Lauder Morton (b. 24th April 1893) - Scottish international footballer and "Wembley Wizard" who played for Queen's Park and Rangers.
16th Dec	Torrance "Torry" Gillick (b. 19th May 1915) - Scottish international footballer who played for Rangers, Everton and Partick Thistle.
21st Dec	Captain Charles Chaplin Banks, DFC, MC (b. 17th December 1893) - World War I flying ace credited with thirteen aerial victories.

1971 TOP 10 SINGLES

George Harrison	No.1	My Sweet Lord
Rod Stewart	No.2	Maggie May / Reason To Believe
Middle Of The Road	No.3	Chirpy Chirpy Cheep Cheep
Dawn	No.4	Knock Three Times
T. Rex	No.5	Hot Love
The Mixtures	No.6	The Pushbike Song
The New Seekers	No.7	Never Ending Song Of Love
Diana Ross	No.8	I'm Still Waiting
The Tams	No.9	Hey Girl Don't Bother Me
T. Rex	No.10	Get It On

 ## George Harrison
My Sweet Lord

Label:	Written by:	Length:
Apple Records	George Harrison	4 mins 39 secs

George Harrison, MBE (b. 25th February 1943 - d. 29th November 2001) was a musician, singer, songwriter, and music and film producer who achieved international fame as the lead guitarist and occasional lead vocalist of the Beatles. Harrison released several best-selling singles and albums as a solo performer and, in 1988, he co-founded the platinum-selling supergroup the Traveling Wilburys. He is a two-time Rock and Roll Hall of Fame inductee - as a member of the Beatles in 1988, and posthumously for his solo career in 2004.

 ## Rod Stewart
Reason To Believe / Maggie May

Label:	Written by:	Length:
Mercury	Quittenton / Stewart	4m 7s / 5m 15s

Sir **Roderick David Stewart**, CBE (b. 10th January 1945) is a rock singer and songwriter who is one of the best-selling music artists of all time having sold over 250 million records worldwide. He has had ten No.1 albums in the British Albums Chart, and his tally of 62 hit singles includes 31 that reached the top ten and six of which gained the No.1 position. Stewart has been inducted twice into the Rock and Roll Hall of Fame; in 1994 as a solo artist, and in 2012 as a member of the rock band Faces.

3 Middle Of The Road
Chirpy Chirpy Cheep Cheep

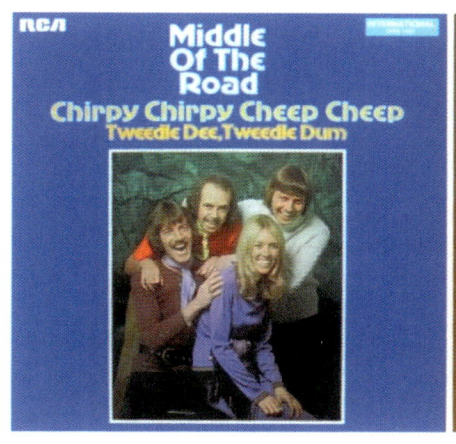

Label:	Written by:	Length:
RCA Victor	Cassia / Stott	2 mins 56 secs

Middle of the Road are a Scottish pop group who have enjoyed success across Europe and Latin America since the 1970s. Before ABBA established themselves in the mid-70s, Middle of the Road were the sound of early europop with their distinctive harmonies and lead vocals from Sally Carr. Four of their singles have sold over one million copies each; Chirpy Chirpy Cheep Cheep, Sacramento, Tweedle Dee Tweedle Dum, and Soley Soley.

---

4 Dawn
Knock Three Times

Label:	Written by:	Length:
Bell Records	Levine / Russell Brown	2 mins 56 secs

Dawn (later billed as Tony Orlando and Dawn) is an American pop music group that was popular in the 1970s. Their signature hits include Candida, Knock Three Times, Tie A Yellow Ribbon Round The Ole Oak Tree, Say, Has Anybody Seen My Sweet Gypsy Rose, and He Don't Love You (Like I Love You). The group was inducted into the Vocal Group Hall of Fame in 2008.

5 T. Rex
Hot Love

Label:	Written by:	Length:
Fly Records	Marc Bolan	4 mins 50 secs

T. Rex were an English rock band formed in 1967 by singer-songwriter and guitarist Marc Bolan (b. Mark Feld; 30th September 1947 - d. 16th September 1977). The band was initially called Tyrannosaurus Rex, and released four psychedelic folk albums under this name. In 1969 Bolan began to change the band's style towards electric rock and shortened their name to T. Rex the following year. This development culminated in 1970's "Ride a White Swan", and the group soon became pioneers of the glam rock movement.

6 The Mixtures
The Pushbike Song

Label:	Written by:	Length:
Polydor	Idris & Evan Jones	2 mins 27 secs

The Mixtures were an Australian rock band that formed in Melbourne in 1965. The Pushbike Song was the first record entirely written, performed and produced in Australia to become an international hit. It reached No.2 in the U.K. at the start of 1971, and stayed in the Top 50 for 21 weeks. It was also released by Sire Records in the USA where it reached No.44 on the Billboard Top 100.

7 The New Seekers
Never Ending Song Of Love

Label:
Philips

Written by:
Delaney / Bramlett

Length:
3 mins 8 secs

The New Seekers are a pop group formed in London in 1969 by Keith Potger after the break-up of his group, The Seekers. They achieved their breakthrough hit, Never Ending Song Of Love, in June 1971, and then went on to gain worldwide success with records such as, I'd Like To Teach The World To Sing, You Won't Find Another Fool Like Me, and Beg, Steal Or Borrow (which came second representing the U.K. in the 1972 Eurovision Song Contest).

8 Diana Ross
I'm Still Waiting

Label:
Tamla Motown

Written by:
Deke Richards

Length:
3 mins 35 secs

Diana Ross (b. 26th March 1944) is a singer, actress and record producer. Ross rose to fame as the lead singer of the vocal group the Supremes, Motown's most successful act. In 1988 Ross was inducted to the Rock and Roll Hall of Fame as a member of the Supremes, and in 2012 received a Grammy Lifetime Achievement Award.

The Tams
Hey Girl Don't Bother Me

Label:	Written by:	Length:
His Master's Voice	Ray Whitley	2 mins 16 secs

The Tams are an American vocal group who enjoyed their greatest chart success in the 1960s, but continued to chart in the 1970s, and the 1980s. The group reached the No.1 slot in the U.K. Singles Chart in September 1971 with the re-issue of "Hey Girl Don't Bother Me", thanks to its initial support from the then thriving Northern soul scene. The song also went to No.1 in Ireland, making them the first black soul group to top the Irish Charts.

T. Rex
Get It On

Label:	Written by:	Length:
Fly Records	Marc Bolan	4 mins 25 secs

From 1970 to 1973, **T. Rex** encountered a popularity in the U.K. comparable to that of the Beatles, with a run of eleven singles in the top ten. They scored four British No.1 hits, Hot Love, Get It On, Telegram Sam and Metal Guru. The band's 1971 album Electric Warrior received critical acclaim as a pioneering glam rock album and also reached No.1 in the U.K. T. Rex were inducted into the Rock and Roll Hall of Fame in 2020.

1971: TOP FILMS

1. **Fiddler on the Roof** - *United Artists*
2. **The French Connection** - *20th Century Fox*
3. **Summer of '42** - *Warner Bros.*
4. **Diamonds Are Forever** - *United Artists*
5. **Dirty Harry** - *Warner Bros.*

OSCARS

Best Picture: The French Connection
Produced by: Philip D'Antoni

Most Nominations: Fiddler on the Roof (8) / The French Connection (8) / The Last Picture Show (8)
Most Wins: The French Connection (5)

Philip D'Antoni / Gene Hackman / Jane Fonda / William Friedkin

Best Director: William Friedkin - *The French Connection*

Best Actor: Gene Hackman - *The French Connection*
Best Actress: Jane Fonda - *Klute*
Best Supporting Actor: Ben Johnson - *The Last Picture Show*
Best Supporting Actress: Cloris Leachman - *The Last Picture Show*

The 44th Academy Awards, honouring the best in film for 1971, were presented on the 10th April 1971 at the Dorothy Chandler Pavilion in Los Angeles, California.

FIDDLER ON THE ROOF

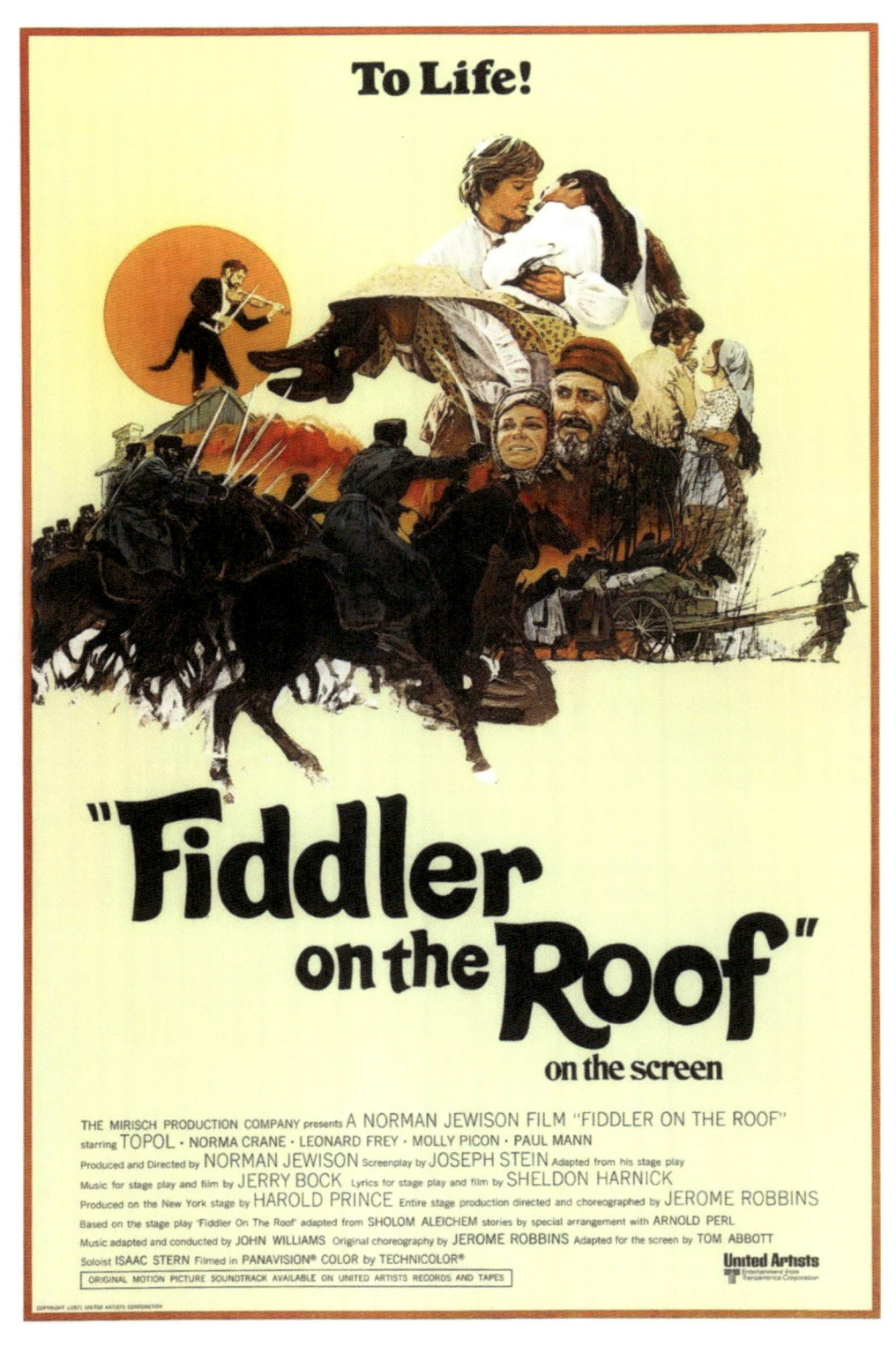

Directed by: Norman Jewison - Runtime: 3h 1m

In pre-revolutionary Russia, a Jewish peasant contends with marrying off three of his daughters whilst growing anti-Semitic sentiment threatens his village.

Starring

Chaim Topol
b. 9th September 1935

Character:
Tevye

Norma Crane
b. 10th November 1928
d. 28th September 1973

Character:
Golde

Leonard Frey
b. 4th September 1938
d. 24th August 1988

Character:
Motel

Trivia

Interesting Facts

Director Norman Jewison was brought into the project by executives at United Artists who thought he was Jewish. His first words to the executives upon meeting them were, "You know I'm not Jewish, right?"

To get the look he wanted for the film, Norman Jewison told director of photography Oswald Morris to shoot the film in an earthy tone. To achieve the effect the entire film was made with a brown nylon stocking placed over the camera lens; Morris went on to win the Oscar for Best Cinematography.

Before production, Norma Crane was diagnosed with breast cancer, which would eventually kill her. She told only director Norman Jewison, co-star Chaim Topol and associate producer Patrick J. Palmer, all of whom kept her secret.

The cart-horse, nicknamed "Shmuel" by the cast, was purchased from a lot destined for a Zagreb glue factory. After production Norman Jewison paid a local farmer to keep him for the rest of his natural life (which turned out to be three years).

Throughout the film, every time Topol talked to God he was actually talking to a white ball on the end of a stick.

Quotes

Perchik: Money is the world's curse.
Tevye: May the Lord smite me with it. And may I never recover.

Tevye: As the good book says, when a poor man eats a chicken, one of them is sick.
Mendel: Where does the book say that?
Tevye: Well, it doesn't say that exactly, but somewhere there is something about a chicken.

The French Connection

Directed by: William Friedkin - Runtime: 1h 44m

A pair of New York City cops stumble onto a drug smuggling job with a French connection.

Starring

Gene Hackman	**Fernando Rey**	**Roy Scheider**
b. 30th January 1930	b. 20th September 1917	b. 10th November 1932
	d. 9th March 1994	d. 10th February 2008
Character:	**Character:**	**Character:**
Jimmy 'Popeye' Doyle	Alain Charnier	Buddy 'Cloudy' Russo

Trivia

Goof — Early on in the film, a Frenchman is shot. The "blood" comes from a hose which squirts red paint at the actor's face and is clearly visible at the bottom of the screen.

Interesting Facts — The film is based on actual events described in the book 'The French Connection: A True Account of Cops, Narcotics, and International Conspiracy' written by Robin Moore in 1969. According to director William Friedkin, the film is an "impression of that case" that took place between the 7th October 1961 and 24th February 1962. Detectives Jimmy Doyle and Buddy Russo were based on the real officers on the case, Eddie Egan and Sonny Grosso. Although their real names were changed for the film, Egan and Grosso were actually nicknamed 'Popeye' and 'Cloudy' like their counterparts in the film.

Roy Scheider and Gene Hackman patrolled with Eddie Egan and Sonny Grosso for a month to get the feel of the characters.

The principal car chase scene was widely considered to be the best ever put on film, overtaking Bullitt (1968) for the honour. William Friedkin later attempted to outdo this with a sequence in To Live and Die in L.A. (1985).

Quote — **Jimmy 'Popeye' Doyle**: I got a man in Poughkeepsie who wants to talk to you. Have you ever been in Poughkeepsie? Huh? Have you ever been in Poughkeepsie?
Brooklyn Drug Dealer: Hey, man, come on, give me a break, man. I don't know what you're talkin' about!
Jimmy 'Popeye' Doyle: Hey, come on, come on. Say it. Let me hear you say it. Come on. Have you ever been to Poughkeepsie? You've been in Poughkeepsie, haven't you? I want to hear it! Come on!
Brooklyn Drug Dealer: Yes. Yes. Yes. I've been there.

SUMMER OF '42

Directed by: Robert Mulligan - **Runtime:** 1h 44m

During his summer vacation on Nantucket Island during World War II, 15-year-old Hermie finds himself falling in love with the married Dorothy, whose husband has recently been sent to the battlefront.

Starring

Jennifer O'Neill
b. 20th February 1948

Character:
Dorothy

Gary Grimes
b. 2nd June 1955

Character:
Hermie

Jerry Houser
b. 14th July 1952

Character:
Oscy

Trivia

Goof | During the film a modern bridge and vehicles can be seen outside the drugstore window near the greeting cards rack. It is also seen when Hermie and Oscy are conversing outside the drugstore.

Interesting Facts | Although author Herman Raucher admits to moving the order of certain events around and interchanging some dialogue, the movie is (according to those involved) an accurate depiction of events in Raucher's life in the summer of 1942 on Nantucket Island; even names have not been changed. He began writing the screenplay as a tribute to his friend Oscy, who had been killed in the Korean War, but midway through writing it Raucher realised that he wanted to make it a story about Dorothy, who he had in fact neither seen nor heard from since their last night together as depicted in the movie. Raucher admits that in all the time he knew her he never bothered to ask her what her last name was.

When it was first released the film was banned in Ireland (until 1980) because the character Hermie is shown buying contraceptives from a drugstore whilst under age (contraception was banned in Ireland until 1980).

A scene from this film (where Hermie helps bring home Dorothy's groceries) appears on television in Stanley Kubrick's "The Shining", simply because Kubrick thought Summer of '42 was such a great film.

Summer of '42 was the only non-Best Picture Oscar nominee for 1971 to be nominated for Best Cinematography.

Quote | **Narrator**: *[voice-over]* Nothing from that first day I saw her and no one that has happened to me since, has ever been as frightening and as confusing. For no person I've ever known has ever done more to make me feel more sure, more insecure, more important and less significant.

DIAMONDS ARE FOREVER

Directed by: Guy Hamilton - Runtime: 1h 41m

A diamond smuggling investigation leads James Bond to Las Vegas where he uncovers an evil plot involving a rich business tycoon.

Starring

Sean Connery
b. 25th August 1930
d. 31st October 2020
Character:
James Bond

Jill St. John
b. 19th August 1940
Character:
Tiffany Case

Charles Gray
b. 28th August 1928
d. 7th March 2000
Character:
Blofeld

Trivia

Goof | When Bond and Tiffany are eluding pursuers by driving down a narrow alley, they manage to tip their Mustang so its balanced on its two right wheels, but when it emerges from the other end, it's on its two left wheels.

Interesting Facts | United Artists paid Sean Connery a then-record $1,250,000 to return as James Bond after George Lazenby left the series.

Diamonds Are Forever was the second of three Bond title songs sung by Shirley Bassey. The others were Goldfinger (1964) and Moonraker (1979). To date, she is the only singer to have performed more than one Bond title song.

Actresses considered for the role of Tiffany Case included Raquel Welch, Jane Fonda and Faye Dunaway. Jill St. John had originally been offered the part of Plenty O'Toole but landed the lead after impressing director Guy Hamilton during screentests. She became the first American Bond Girl.

Producers Harry Saltzman and Albert R. Broccoli cast Lana Wood as Plenty O'Toole after seeing her in Playboy Magazine. Her voice was dubbed in the movie, and she is standing on a box for some of her scenes with Sean Connery because, even in high heels, she was still too small to fit into the frame with him.

Quotes | *[while fumbling inside the pipeline, Bond sees a rat]*
James Bond: Well, one of us smells like a tart's handkerchief.
James Bond: *[sniffs]* I'm afraid it's me. Sorry, old boy.

James Bond: Felix, if she gives your men the slip...
Felix Leiter: Relax, I've got upwards of 30 agents down there. A mouse with sneakers on couldn't get through.

DIRTY HARRY

Dirty Harry and the homicidal maniac.

Harry's the one with the badge.

Clint Eastwood
Dirty Harry

Directed by: Don Siegel - Runtime: 1h 42m

Tough as nails San Francisco Police Inspector "Dirty" Harry Callahan is assigned to track down a psychopathic sniper called the Scorpio Killer.

Starring

Clint Eastwood
b. 31st May 1930

Character:
Harry Callahan

Harry Guardino
b. 23rd December 1925
d. 17th July 1995

Character:
Bressler

Reni Santoni
b. 21st April 1938
d. 1st August 2020

Character:
Chico

Trivia

Goofs | When Harry is following Scorpio's instructions to run from phone booth to phone booth, he boards the subway. When he arrives at his destination it is the same station as the one he started out from.

The family portrait showing two children, in the offices of both Lt. Bressler and District Attorney Rothko, are the same.

Interesting Facts | Serial killer Scorpio was loosely based on the Zodiac killer who used to taunt police and media with notes about his crimes. The role of Harry Callahan was loosely based on real-life detective David Toschi, who was the chief investigator on the Zodiac case.

When Harry finally meets Scorpio in Mount Davidson Park, Scorpio orders him to show his gun with his left hand. Harry pulls it from his holster and Scorpio ad-libs the line, "My, that's a big one!" This line caused the crew to crack up and the scene had to be re-shot, but the line stayed.

The Scorpio Killer's real name is never revealed throughout the entire film and in the ending credits he is simply listed as "killer". However, after the film's release, a novelisation gave his real name as Charles Davis.

This success of Dirty Harry led to the development of the television show The Streets of San Francisco (1972-1977).

Quote | **Harry Callahan:** Uh uh. I know what you're thinking. "Did he fire six shots or only five?" Well to tell you the truth in all this excitement I kinda lost track myself. But being this is a .44 Magnum, the most powerful handgun in the world and would blow your head clean off, you've gotta ask yourself one question: Do I feel lucky? Well, do ya, punk?

SPORTING WINNERS

BBC SPORTS PERSONALITY OF THE YEAR

Pictured: Princess Anne riding her horse Doublet in the 1971 Eridge Horse Trials, and receiving her Sports Personality of the Year Award from Henry Cooper.

1971	BBC Sports Personality	Country	Sport
Winner	**Princess Anne**	**England**	**Eventing**
Runner Up	George Best	Northern Ireland	Football
Third Place	Barry John	Wales	Rugby Union

PRINCESS ANNE - EVENTING

Anne, Princess Royal, KG, KT, GCVO, GCStJ, QSO, CD (Anne Elizabeth Alice Louise; b. 15th August 1950) is the second child and only daughter of Queen Elizabeth II and Prince Philip, Duke of Edinburgh.

Although Princess Anne is now known for her high-profile charity work, which involves her patronage of more than 200 organisations, in her youth she was known for her equestrianism. In later years she also notably assumed the Presidency of the Fédération Équestre Internationale (1986-1994). *Fun fact: Princess Anne was the first member of the British royal family to compete in an Olympic Games - 1976, Montreal.*

Equestrianism Record:

European Championships	Event	Medal
Burghley (1971)	Individual Eventing	Gold
Luhmuhlen (1975)	Team Eventing	Silver
Luhmuhlen (1975)	Individual Eventing	Silver

Five Nations Rugby
Wales

Position	Nation	Played	Won	Draw	Lost	For	Against	+/-	Points
1	**Wales**	4	4	0	0	73	38	+35	8
2	France	4	1	2	1	41	40	+1	4
3	Ireland	4	1	1	2	41	46	-5	3
4	England	4	1	1	2	44	58	-14	3
5	Scotland	4	1	0	3	47	64	-17	2

The 1971 and forty-second series of the rugby union Five Nations Championship saw ten matches played between the 16th January and the 27th March. Including the previous incarnations as the Home Nations and Five Nations, this was the seventy-seventh series of the northern hemisphere rugby union championship, and the last where a try was worth 3 points. The competition saw Wales win their seventeenth title, their twelfth Triple Crown, and saw them complete the Grand Slam for the first time since 1952.

Date	Team	Score	Team	Location
16-01-1971	France	13-8	Scotland	Paris
16-01-1971	Wales	22-6	England	Cardiff
30-01-1971	Ireland	9-9	France	Dublin
06-02-1971	Scotland	18-19	Wales	Edinburgh
13-02-1971	Ireland	6-9	England	Dublin
27-02-1971	Scotland	5-17	Ireland	Edinburgh
27-02-1971	England	14-14	France	London
13-03-1971	Wales	23-9	Ireland	Cardiff
20-03-1971	England	15-16	Scotland	London
27-03-1971	France	5-9	Wales	Paris

Calcutta Cup
England 15-16 Scotland

The Calcutta Cup was first awarded in 1879 and is the rugby union trophy awarded to the winner of the match (currently played as part of the Six Nations Championship) between England and Scotland. The Cup was presented to the Rugby Football Union after the Calcutta Football Club in India disbanded in 1878; it is made from melted down silver rupees withdrawn from the club's funds.

Historical Records: England 71 wins / Scotland 40 wins / 16 draws

British Grand Prix

Jackie Stewart in his race winning Tyrrell-Ford at the 1971 British Grand Prix.

The 1971 British Grand Prix was held at Silverstone on the 17th July and was won by Tyrrell driver Jackie Stewart (from second position) over 68 laps of the 2.927-mile circuit.

Pos.	Country	Driver	Car
1	**United Kingdom**	**Jackie Stewart**	**Tyrrell-Ford**
2	Sweden	Ronnie Peterson	March-Ford
3	Brazil	Emerson Fittipaldi	Lotus-Ford

1971 Grand Prix Season

Date	Grand Prix	Circuit	Winning Driver	Constructor
06-03	South African	Kyalami	Mario Andretti	Ferrari
18-04	Spanish	Montjuïc	Jackie Stewart	Tyrrell-Ford
23-05	Monaco	Monaco	Jackie Stewart	Tyrrell-Ford
20-06	Dutch	Zandvoort	Jacky Ickx	Ferrari
04-07	French	Paul Ricard	Jackie Stewart	Tyrrell-Ford
17-07	British	Silverstone	Jackie Stewart	Tyrrell-Ford
01-08	German	Nürburgring	Jackie Stewart	Tyrrell-Ford
15-08	Austrian	Österreichring	Jo Siffert	BRM
05-09	Italian	Monza	Peter Gethin	BRM
19-09	Canadian	Mosport Park	Jackie Stewart	Tyrrell-Ford
03-10	United States	Watkins Glen	François Cevert	Tyrrell-Ford

The 1971 Formula One season was the twenty-fifth season of FIA Formula One motor racing. Jackie Stewart won the championship for the United Kingdom with 62 points, from Ronnie Peterson (Sweden, 33 points) and François Cevert (France, 26 points).

GRAND NATIONAL SPECIFY

The 1971 Grand National was the 125th renewal of this world famous horse race and took place at Aintree Racecourse near Liverpool on the 3rd April. The winning horse was Specify who was trained by John Sutcliffe and owned by Pontins holiday camp founder Fred Pontin. Of the 38 runners only 13 horses completed the course; 14 fell, 4 were brought down, 3 pulled up, 3 refused and 1 unseated its rider. *Photo: Specify being led into the paddock after the winning the Grand National.*

	Horse	Jockey	Age	Weight	Odds
1st	**Specify**	**John Cook**	9	**10st-3lb**	28/1
2nd	Black Secret	Jim Dreaper	7	11st-5lb	20/1
3rd	Astbury	Jimmy Bourke	8	10st-0lb	33/1

EPSOM DERBY - MILL REEF

The Derby Stakes is Britain's richest horse race and the most prestigious of the country's five Classics. First run in 1780 this Group 1 flat horse race is open to 3-year-old thoroughbred colts and fillies. The race takes place at Epsom Downs in Surrey over a distance of one mile, four furlongs and 10 yards (2,423 metres) and is scheduled for early June each year.

The 1971 Derby was won by Mill Reef, ridden by jockey Geoff Lewis. In his short career (1970-1972) Mill Reef won twelve of his fourteen races earning £309,225.

Photo: Champion Thoroughbred racehorse and sire Mill Reef (1968-1986) with breeder and owner Paul Mellon after winning the 1971 Epsom Derby.

Football League Champions

England

Pos.	Team	W	D	L	F	A	Pts.
1	**Arsenal**	**29**	**7**	**6**	**71**	**29**	**65**
2	Leeds United	27	10	5	72	30	64
3	Tottenham Hotspur	19	14	9	54	33	52
4	Wolverhampton Wanderers	22	8	12	64	54	52
5	Liverpool	17	17	8	42	24	51

Scotland

Pos.	Team	W	D	L	F	A	Pts.
1	**Celtic**	**25**	**6**	**3**	**89**	**23**	**56**
2	Aberdeen	24	6	4	68	18	54
3	St Johnstone	19	6	9	59	44	44
4	Rangers	16	9	9	58	34	41
5	Dundee	14	10	10	53	45	38

FA Cup Winners - Arsenal

Liverpool 1-2 Arsenal

The 1971 FA Cup Final took place on the 8th May at Wembley Stadium in front of 100,000 fans. Arsenal won 2-1 after extra time, with all three goals coming in the added half-hour. Steve Heighway scored for Liverpool first, before Arsenal equalised with a goal from substitute Eddie Kelly (the first time a substitute had ever scored in an FA Cup final). Charlie George scored the winner shortly after. *Photo: Arsenal's Charlie George and captain Frank McLintock holding the FA Cup aloft after their victory against Liverpool.*

SNOOKER - JOHN SPENCER

John Spencer   37-29   Warren Simpson

The 1971 World Snooker Championship was held in 1970, between the 28th September and 7th November, at the Chevron Hotel in Sydney, Australia. John Spencer knocked out defending champion Ray Reardon in the semi-final and went on to win the event for the second time, defeating Warren Simpson 37-29 in the final. Eddie Charlton made the highest break of the tournament with a 129.

GOLF - OPEN CHAMPIONSHIP - LEE TREVINO

The 1971 Open Championship was the 100th to be played and was held between the 7th and 10th July at Royal Birkdale Golf Club in Southport, England. Lee Trevino won the first of his consecutive Open Championships, one stroke ahead of Lu Liang-Huan, to take home the £5,500 winners share of the £45,000 prize fund. This was the third of Trevino's six major titles.

WIMBLEDON

Men's Singles Champion - John Newcombe - Australia
Ladies Singles Champion - Evonne Goolagong - Australia

The 1971 Wimbledon Championships was the 85th staging of tournament and took place on the outdoor grass courts at the All England Lawn Tennis and Croquet Club in Wimbledon, London. It ran from the 21st June until the 3rd July, and was the third Grand Slam tennis event of 1971.

Men's Singles Final:

Country	Player	Set 1	Set 2	Set 3	Set 4	Set 5
Australia	John Newcombe	6	5	2	6	6
United States	Stan Smith	3	7	6	4	4

Women's Singles Final:

Country	Player	Set 1	Set 2
Australia	Evonne Goolagong	6	6
Australia	Margaret Court	4	1

Men's Doubles Final:

Country	Players	Set 1	Set 2	Set 3	Set 4	Set 5
Australia	Roy Emerson / Rod Laver	4	9	6	6	6
United States	Arthur Ashe / Dennis Ralston	6	7	8	4	4

Women's Doubles Final:

Country	Players	Set 1	Set 2
United States	Rosie Casals / Billie Jean King	6	6
Australia	Margaret Court / Evonne Goolagong	3	2

Mixed Doubles Final:

Country	Players	Set 1	Set 2	Set 3
Australia / United States	Owen Davidson / Billie Jean King	3	6	15
United States / Australia	Marty Riessen / Margaret Court	6	2	13

County Championship Cricket - Surrey

1971 saw the seventy-second officially organised running of the County Championship. Surrey won the Championship title over Warwickshire (even though they had finished level on points) by virtue of winning more matches.

Pos.	Team	Played	Won	Lost	Drawn	Batting Bonus	Bowling Bonus	Points
1	**Surrey**	**24**	**11**	**3**	**10**	**63**	**82**	**255**
2	Warwickshire	24	9	9	6	73	92	255
3	Lancashire	24	9	4	11	76	75	241
4	Kent	24	7	6	11	82	82	234
5	Leicestershire	24	6	2	16	76	74	215

Test Series

England 1-0 Pakistan
1st Test: Match drawn
2nd Test: Match drawn
3rd Test: England win by 25 runs

Test	Ground / Date	Innings	Team	Score	Overs	Team	Score	Overs
1st	Edgbaston 03/06 - 08/06	1st	Pakistan	608/7d	195	England	353	120.5
		2nd	Pakistan	-	-	England	229/5	90.5
2nd	Lord's 17/06 - 22/06	1st	England	241/2d	83	Pakistan	148	72.4
		2nd	England	117/0	45	Pakistan	-	-
3rd	Headingley 08/07 - 13/07	1st	England	316	105.2	Pakistan	350	209.4
		2nd	England	264	107.3	Pakistan	205	88.3

England 0-1 India
1st Test: Match drawn
2nd Test: Match drawn
3rd Test: India win by 4 wickets

Test	Ground / Date	Innings	Team	Score	Overs	Team	Score	Overs
1st	Lord's 22/07 - 27/07	1st	England	304	139.3	India	313	165.3
		2nd	England	191	98.5	India	145/8	50
2nd	Old Trafford 05/08 - 10/08	1st	England	386	160.4	India	212	93
		2nd	England	245/3d	66	India	65/3	27
3rd	Kennington Oval 19/08 - 24/08	1st	England	355	108.4	India	284	117.3
		2nd	England	101	45.1	India	174/6	101

COST OF LIVING

COMPARISON CHART

	1971	1971 (+ Inflation)	2020	% Change
3 Bedroom House	£5,940	£92,729	£234,853	+153.3%
Weekly Income	£14.81	£231.17	£619	+167.8%
Pint Of Beer	8p	£1.11	£3.79	+241.4%
Cheese (lb)	33p	£5.14	£2.98	-42.0%
Bacon (lb)	40p	£6.11	£2.94	-51.9%
The Beano	2p	26p	£2.75	+957.7%

FOOD & DRINK

Large Loaf Of Bread	10p
Country Life Butter (½lb)	11½p
Stork Margarine (½lb)	6½p
Large White Eggs (dozen)	25p
Pint Of Milk	5p
Nescafe Coffee (8oz)	47½p
Coca Cola (can)	5½p
Golden Wonder Crisps	3p
Haig Whisky	£2.53

Mini £723 **Hot Mini £732**

A lot of you may prefer not to think about the British winter.

Particularly if you don't happen to have a heated rear window on your car.

During the colder months, the early morning scrape can become as regular as the morning shave.

So it'll come as a pleasant surprise to find out how very inexpensive a factory-fitted Triplex Hotline can be.

Less than £10 on the Mini, for instance. At that sort of price, you shouldn't make the same mistake on your next new car.

And on cold, misty, frosty mornings, you'll be avoiding a lot of tough scrapes.

XXX Triplex

Triplex Hotline. The essential option.
For leaflet contact Triplex Safety Glass Co. Ltd., 1 Albemarle St., London W.1. Tel: 01-493 8171.

CLOTHES

Women's Clothing

Quilted Nylon Car Coat	£2.50
Maytime Hand Made Model Hat	£2.20
Andre De Brett Crimplene Trouser Suit	£1.67
Georgina Ribbed Polyester Dress	£3.50
Trendsetters Pinafore Dress	£3.10
R. J. Wiltshire ¾ Lined Skirt	£1.40
Crimplene Polyester Mini-Skirt	£1.25
R. J. Wiltshire Flared Slacks	£2.50
Gayfurs Suede Hot Pants	£2.80
Brentford's Quilted Dressing Gown	£1.99
Brentford's Elegant Nighties (x2)	£1.99
Value Nylon Corselette	£3.45
Ballito Pantee Hose & Girdle	£1.30
Inch Trim Hotpants	£4.50
Pretty Polly Eve Tights	£4.90
Bury Boot Summer Shoe	£2.75

Beat our prices – if you can!

HALWINS POSTAL BARGAINS SAVE YOU £££'S—UNBEATABLE VALUE AT UNREPEATABLE PRICES. AND A 14-DAY MONEY-BACK GUARANTEE IF YOU'RE NOT COMPLETELY SATISFIED

Button thro' CRIMPLENE Mididress High fashion styling. Super loop button fastening. Colour: Black. Hip Sizes: 34, 36, 38, 40, 42. Order No. S4. **ONLY £1.35**

High Fashion CRIMPLENE Trouser Suit. Neat, sleeveless Crimplene jerkin and trouser suit with "snakeskin" band and tab fasteners. Pants to match with front fly zip. Hip Sizes: 34, 36, 38, 40, 42. Colours: Black/White. Order No. S1. **ONLY £2.00**

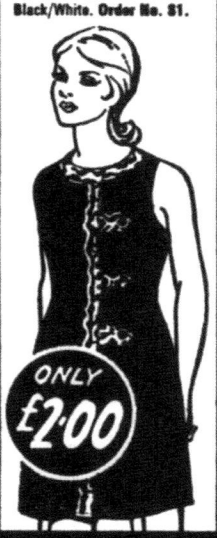

100% Nylon Shirt. Stylish fine check on white ground. Sizes 14½, 15, 15½. Order No. S5. **ONLY 60p**

Polo Neck Jumper. In 100% pure wool. Colour: Turquoise. Sizes: 36, 38, 40. Order No. S8. **ONLY £1.25**

FILL IN THIS ORDER FORM NOW AND POST TO: HALWINS LTD. BENFLEET, ESSEX SS7 5SG

Please send me the following cash bargains

Order No	Quantity	Colour	Size	Price Each	Total £ p

Add postage and packing (all orders) 10p.
I enclose crossed cheque/postal order No ....
payable to Halwins Ltd for £ ....

Name _____ (BLOCK LETTERS, PLEASE)
Address _____

Halwins 1971/72 Autumn/Winter Catalogue is packed with 100's of fantastic bargain buys.
☐ Tick box for your FREE copy.

HALWINS FOR BEST BARGAIN BUYS

Men's Clothing

Jacatex Winter Casual Coat	£4.98
Ex-Govt Melton Reefer Coat	£3.98
Western Warehouse Heavyweight Sweater	£1.30
Solar Supplies Heavy Duty Work Shirt	95p
Halwins Nylon Shirt	60p
Mr. John Long Sleeve Button Vest	£1
A. K. Trading Police Trousers	£1.98
C&A Washable Corduroy Jeans	£1.25
Brentford's Quilted Dressing Gown	£2.50
Brentford's Nylon Pyjamas	£1.50
Leathercraft Shoes	£4.25

Booth's & Cola

Say Booth's first.
And discover a fine edge of flavour that makes all the difference to tonic, cola, bitter lemon, soda, orange, lime, ginger beer, sweet or dry vermouth.
Always put Booth's first, when you want something really different to happen.

Booth's Gin. Experience it soon.

TOYS

Space Hopper	£2.25
MFI Two Room Playhouse	£2.95
Giant Cuddly Teddy	£2.25
Sandy - Walking, Talking, Singing Doll	£7.99
Weebles	£4.99
Lego Fire Station & Engine	£2.65
Mastermind Board Game	£1.64
Travel Scrabble	£1.69
Thunderbird 2 Dinky Toy	95p
Etch A Sketch	99p

BE FIRST IN YOUR GANG WITH JOE'S CAR

*ANOTHER WINNER FROM DINKY TOYS®

UNIQUE ACTION FEATURES IN JOE'S CAR
1. Automatic opening wings
2. Extending tail fins
3. Flashing engine exhaust
4. Independent super suspension
5. Plated twin aero turbine engines
6. Jewelled headlights

IN YOUR TOYSHOPS NOW! MODEL No.102

DIRECT FROM JOE 90

MORE DINKY TOYS FROM YOUR TV FAVOURITES

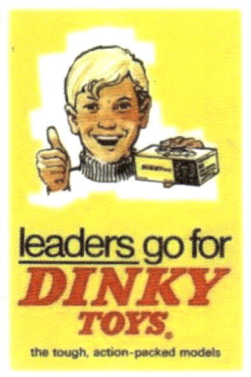

CAPTAIN SCARLET'S TERRIFIC TRIO — DIRECT FROM CAPTAIN SCARLET AND THE MYSTERONS
- Spectrum Pursuit Vehicle. Model No. 104
- Spectrum Patrol Car. Model No. 103
- Maximum Security Vehicle. Model No. 105

Lady Penelope's Fab 1 Model No. 100
Two fabulous models from THUNDERBIRDS
Thunderbird 2. Model No. 101

leaders go for DINKY TOYS®
the tough, action-packed models

ELECTRICAL ITEMS

25" HMV Colourmaster Colour TV	£289
24" Ferguson B&W TV	£69
Lewis Four Band AM/FM Radiogram	£59.60
Prinz Sound System 6 Stereo Hi-Fi Outfit	£59.50
Prinz Sound Cassette Recorder	£17.50
Portable Communications & Radio Receiver	£11.97
Hollandia De Luxe Spin Dryer	£16.50
Servis Supertwin MK70 Washing Machine	£84.95
Hollandia De Luxe Vacuum Cleaner	£15.50
Super 8 Magnon LV Film Projector	£36.85
Dixons Concord Rotary Slide Projector	£19.95
Shopertunities Portable Electronic Organ	£7.97
Philips Hood Hair Dryer	£6.30
Westinghouse Hair Curler Set	£5.95
Remmington Selectric Travel Pack Shaver	£8.95
Black & Decker 2-Speed Power Drill	£7.60
Black & Decker Power Hedge Trimmer	£8.80
Imperial Trading Heat Light	£1.40

The Suffolk Super Colt cuts your lawn down to size.

- 12" cut for medium size lawns.
- 5-bladed Sheffield steel cutting cylinder.
- Diecast aluminium side plates to reduce overall weight.
- Dual drive control operated from handle.
- One-piece bottom blade assembly.
- Suffolk 75G 4-stroke engine.
- Extra large metal grassbox.

£29·25
(complete with grassbox)

Qualcast FULLY GUARANTEED

QUALCAST (LAWN MOWERS) LIMITED, SUNNYHILL AVENUE, DERBY DE3 7JT. TELEPHONE: 0332 21021

MOTOR VEHICLES

Jaguar E-Type V12	£3,139
BMW 2000	£2,199
Morris Marina Coupe	£923
Bedford HA Van	£534
Gallon Of Petrol	34p
17ft x 9ft Concrete Garage	£55.90

Spacious Luxury Accommodation
for five people.
UNINTERRUPTED VISION ALL ROUND.
BEAUTIFULLY APPOINTED WITH FITTED CARPETS AND FOAM UNDERLAY THROUGHOUT.
UNIQUE LIGHTING POSSIBILITIES — EVEN ROUND CORNERS.
INFINITE HEATING AND FRESH-AIR CONTROL.
LOW FUEL BILLS.
MONOSHELL STEEL CONSTRUCTION.
FRONT-WHEEL DRIVE.
BRILLIANT PERFORMANCE.
EXCLUSIVE CITROEN HYDROPNEUMATIC SUSPENSION FOR INCOMPARABLE COMFORT AND ROAD HOLDING.
MICHELIN XAS RADIALS ALL ROUND.

You can own a Citroen 'D' Special for £1524·56 (ex. works inc. p.t.) — and there are 12 other 'D' models to choose from. Upkeep is assured by nation-wide network of Citroen Appointed Agents.

The advanced specification of all 'D' Models includes:- Hydropneumatic self-levelling suspension – front wheel drive – full power operated brakes – precise rack and pinion steering (power assistance is standard or optional) – Michelin XAS radial tyres – full five seat interior – monoshell body with detachable panels – optional self-levelling main headlights and directional auxiliary headlights, all quartz iodine – reclining front seats (except FAMILIALE) – electronic tachometer and trip odometer – automatic jack and clearance control – stainless steel trim – heater and demister.

CITROËN

See them at your Citroen agent or write for brochures now. Citroen Cars Ltd., Slough, Bucks. Tel: 23811

Superbly built commuter's paradise.

CITROËN GS WINS CAR OF THE YEAR AWARD 1971

Miscellaneous Items

Spain 15 Days Costa Brava	£38
France 10 Days St. Aygulf	£40.95
Switzerland 10 Days Interlaken	£29
Italy 15 Days Cattolica	£36
7ft x 3ft Wrought Iron Gates	£3.75
American Style Greenhouse	£14.95
Qualcast Superlite Panther Roller Mower	£9.95
MFI Stainless Steel Sink Unit	£9.95
Solid Afro-Teak Monogram Fire Surround	£5.75
Witney Furniture Co. 4ft 6in Divan Bed	£17.75
MFI Junior Safety Bed	£6.95
Luxury Quilted Double Mattress	£9.95
Plumbs Single Continental Quilt	£7.95
Brentford's Nylon Fitted Sheet	£1.50
Daniel De Leo Velvet Rich Nylon Curtains	£2.62
Shackeltons Tapestry Original High Seat	£15.75
Cushionaire Inflatable Armchair	£2.95
Bell Esiplay Accordion	£22.90
Prinz Sabre Automatic Cine Camera	£25.95
Prinz 8x30 Binoculars	£6.30
Rank Aldis Ranger 35 Camera	£22.95
Penn's Decimal Adding Machine	£4.50
Woman's Own Magazine	5p
Daily Mirror Newspaper	3p
Daily Express Newspaper	3p

POOLS GO DECIMAL

NEXT SATURDAY FEB. 20TH.

...JUST AS EASY TO FILL IN YOUR COUPON

THE NEW TREBLE CHANCE STAKES ARE AS FOLLOWS

LITTLEWOODS..... ½ NEW PENNY A LINE
VERNONS.............. ⅛ NEW PENNY A LINE
COPE'S................. 1/16 NEW PENNY A LINE
EMPIRE................. 1/16 NEW PENNY A LINE
ZETTERS.............. 1/20 NEW PENNY A LINE
SOCCER................ 1/20 NEW PENNY A LINE

PPA

Members of the Pool Promoters Association.

BIGGER DIVIDENDS TO BE WON!

CARTOONS & COMIC STRIPS

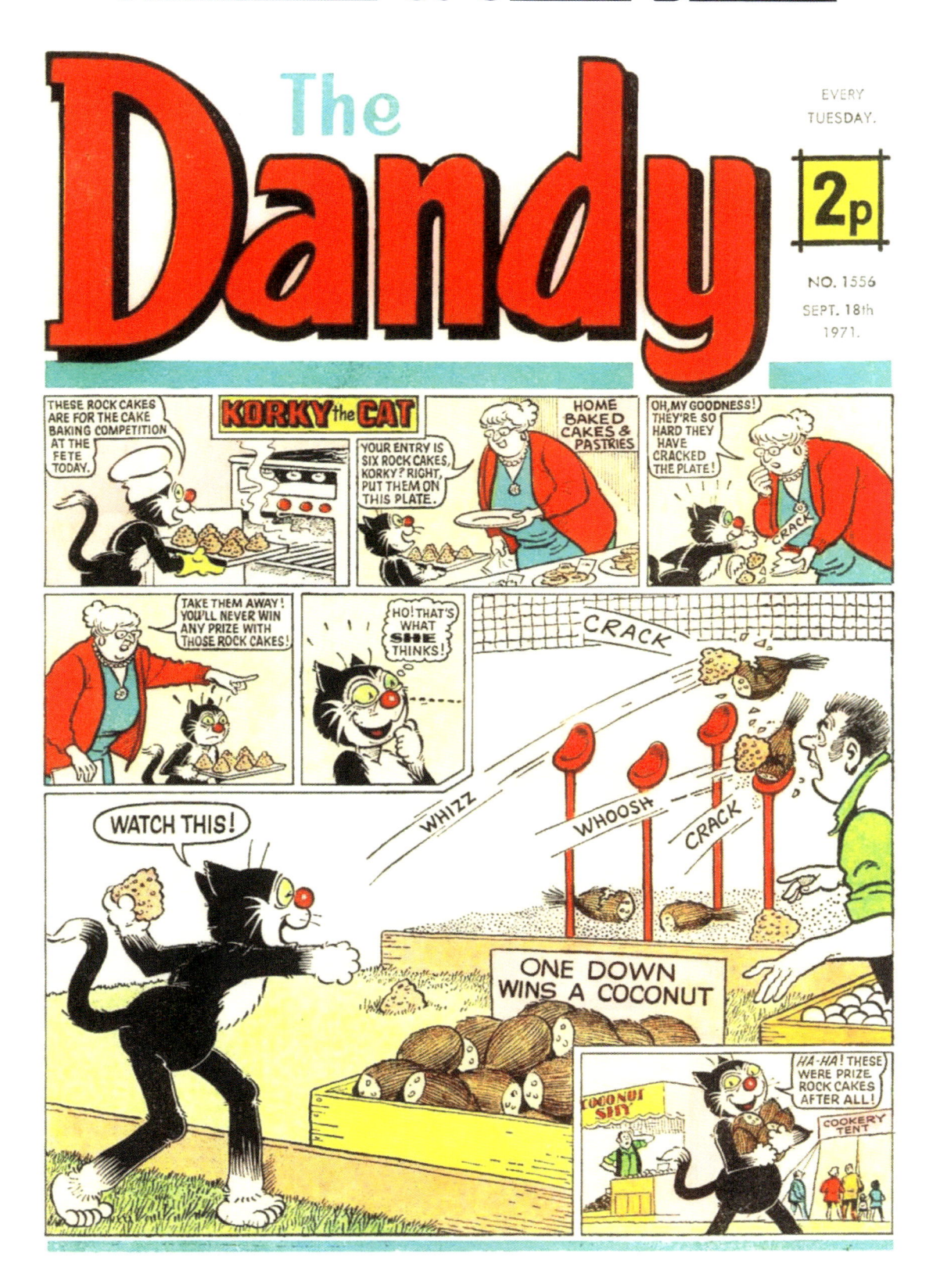

"I told you not to put down 'brain surgeon,' now they've found you a job."

"Now, suppose you decided to make Fricassee de Poulet au Chablis "

THE LARKS

Printed in Great Britain
by Amazon